Indoor Gardening for Beginners

How to Grow Beautiful Plants, Herbs and
Vegetables in your House

Timothy S. Morris

Table of Contents

It Doesn't Matter Where You Live...You Can Start a Garden Right Now

Chapter One: Planning for Success

Choosing a Good Spot

Who Turned Off the Lights?

Airflow

Temperature

Indoor Gardening Methods Exposed

Container Gardening

Herb Gardening

Vertical Gardening Secrets Revealed

Hydroponics Made Easy

Chapter Two: Choosing the Right Soil

What is Compost Anyway?

Mixing it Up

Seem Like Too Much Work?

Chapter Three: Not All Light is the Same

    Incandescent Bulbs

    Fluorescent Bulbs

    Full-Spectrum Fluorescent Bulbs

    LED Lights

    High Intensity Discharge (HID) Bulbs

    How Much Light Do You Need?

Chapter Four: To Water or Not to Water?

Chapter Five: The DIY Herb Garden

Chapter Six: The Versatility of Vertical Gardening

    But Wait...There's More

    The DIY Vertical Garden

    Additional Tips

Chapter Seven: Hydroponics Made Easy

    Four Hydroponic Methods to Consider

    Commercial vs. Homemade Systems

Nine Steps to Building and Maintaining a Bubbling Hydroponic Setup

Chapter Eight: Making a Miniature Ecosystem

What Exactly is Aquaponics?

The Benefits of Aquaponics

The Specifics of an Aquaponics System

Plants to Grow

DIY Aquaponics System

Constructing the System

Chapter Nine: Top 10 Indoor Gardening Tips & Tricks

Chapter 10: Choosing the Right Plants

Vertical Gardening Crops

It Doesn't Matter Where You Live…You Can Start a Garden Right Now

Gardening usually stirs up thoughts of large outdoor setups complete with irrigation systems, fences to keep animals out and row upon row of produce growing in soil perfectly cultivated to provide maximum crop yields.

Gardens like this are still very popular around the world and are an excellent way to become more self-sufficient by growing your own fresh fruits and vegetables at home.

Unfortunately, traditional outdoor gardens also presents a few drawbacks. They take up a lot of space and the growing season can vary by months depending on the region.

For years, I lived in a small apartment without access to land to grow my own food. Everything I ate was purchased at the store — sometimes from questionable sources and often treated with harmful chemicals to increase shelf life. That was, of course, until I learned how to maximize the space all around me. That is to say, the indoor space inside my very own apartment.

But growing food indoors isn't just for apartment dwellers. By growing indoors, you effectively extend the growing season by months. In fact, when properly set up, most indoor gardens can be cultivated year-round. Try doing that outside in the winter months!

Even if you already have an outdoor garden, you should still consider starting some plants indoors. Not only does this allow you to increase annual crop yields, but it may also give you the opportunity to try growing new fruits and vegetables that might not grow in an outdoor environment (depending on where you live).

Basically, the benefits of indoor gardening are:

- Ease and low-cost associated with getting started
- Takes up very little space in the home
- Extends the growing season and even allows for year-round crop production
- Did I mention how easy indoor gardening is?

Even if you have never planted a single crop in your life, I'm going to teach you how to grow beautiful and nutritious fruit and vegetable plants in the comfort of your own home or apartment. Don't think you have enough space? Or enough time to tend the garden?

Sorry to be so blunt, but you're wrong. This book teaches you how to grow your own food using innovative space-saving techniques that, once properly set up, need very little care on a daily basis.

You can do this and this book was specifically designed to give you the knowledge required for instant success.

So, without further ado, let's start a garden!

Chapter One: Planning for Success

Like most things in life, we need to take time when planning our garden to ensure optimal results. Don't worry though, it's really not that difficult.

To properly plan out an indoor garden, keep in mind:

- Location
- Growing method(s)
- Availability of natural light
- Airflow
- Temperature

Now, let's take a look at each of these considerations in more detail.

Choosing a Good Spot

The whole point of indoor gardening is to maximize available space using a variety of growing methods. This is great news because it means we don't need to devote an entire room to gardening (although you certainly can).

Your indoor garden can go anywhere you want — that's the beauty of it. That said, there are few things to consider. How much food you want to grow dictates how much space you should devote to the garden.

A small herb garden is right at home on a window sill in most cases, but larger vegetable plants are better placed in a container where they have enough room to grow. We need to keep the vertical space required by each plant in mind as well as the size of the root system under the soil. This is especially true for root vegetables.

Who Turned Off the Lights?

Perhaps one of the greatest challenges when gardening indoors is ensuring your plants receive the correct amount of light every day. In a traditional outdoor garden, the sun provides up to 12 - 18 hours of sunlight each day during the summer months and many plants, like tomatoes, require lots and lots of sunlight to yield edible food.

The problem, of course, is that the sun moves throughout the day so the likelihood of exposing your plants to enough natural light indoors is slim. All hope isn't lost, however, because if we remember that the sun spends most of the day in the southern sky, we can maximize our plants' access to natural light by placing them near southern facing windows.

Especially when combined with plant species not requiring a lot of sunlight, you may be able to rely on the sun's natural light for most of the year. In the winter, the sun is much lower on the horizon which could prevent some plants from thriving indoors during the off-season.

If you plan to use natural light, find a large southern facing window where the garden can be kept. Also keep in mind any obstacles that could obstruct sunlight during the day (buildings, trees, etc.). By observing the pattern of the sun for a day or two, you should be able to pick out the best spot pretty easily.

Unfortunately for many of us, there isn't enough natural light to support many of the common plant species we want to grow. This means we need to add artificial lighting to supplement the needs of our garden. We're going to talk about artificial grow lights in Chapter Three.

Airflow

Plants survive by converting carbon dioxide in the atmosphere into oxygen. To ensure the garden always has access to carbon dioxide, we need to make sure the are we choose for our garden has sufficient airflow.

If the garden is located in a large, centralized area of the home you really don't have to worry about airflow. There should be plenty. If, on the other hand, the garden is located in a closet or in some other out-of-the-way place, improper airflow is a concern.

The easiest way to overcome this is to add a fan. A simple box fan for the local big-box store is sufficient to move air over even large indoor gardening setups. Just be careful not to turn up the fan too high as this will damage many plants. A slow, gentle breeze is all that's required for optimal airflow.

Temperature

Most plants are picky when it comes to temperature. Although most species can tolerate slight dips in temperature (like those experienced at night in outdoor gardens), continuous exposure to temperatures that are either too hot or too cold will kill your plants or, at the very least, adversely affect crop yield.

Indoor gardening almost completely eliminates concerns about temperature from the equation because I'm assuming the inside temperature of your home remains relatively consistent.

There are a couple of temperature-related considerations that do affect indoor gardens.

Avoid putting your garden near objects that get extraordinarily hot (or cold for that matter). The oven, heaters and the air conditioner are all potential enemies of your plants.

Also keep your garden away from drafty windows and doors in the winter months. Constant bursts of cold air could stunt the growth of plants and significantly reduce yields.

Indoor Gardening Methods Exposed

One of the best parts about indoor gardening is just how many more options we have compared to traditional outdoor gardening techniques. These techniques are easy-to-use, versatile and greatly increase your chances of success the first time around.

Container Gardening

By far the easiest way to start gardening indoors is container gardening. It is inexpensive and with the exception of soil and fertilizer, you probably already have a lot of useable containers lying around your home that you probably don't realize.

Milk jugs, plastic soda bottles, baskets with a plastic liner and mason jars can all be used as containers for your indoor garden. Of course, there are also plenty of commercially-available options too. Window sill planter boxes are a popular way to grow small plants and herbs. More traditional ceramic containers are also an option. These containers are usually more expensive, but the large variety of available sizes make them a convenient choice for many indoor gardening tasks.

You can even make your own containers using wood. For best results, I recommend using either redwood or cedar when making your own planting containers as both species are naturally rot resistant — circumventing the addition of harmful wood treatments which leach into soil and ultimately, your crop.

Herb Gardening

Essentially a variation of container gardening, herb gardening is, well...growing herbs indoors. Herbs are extremely hardy for the most part and take up very little space. This makes for a perfect introduction into the world of indoor gardening. Not only are any excellent culinary tool, but many of them are also useful as alternative medicine, homeopathic supplements and even natural insect repellent (just to name a few).

An indoor herb garden is right at home on a windowsill or in another area with at least five hours of sunlight each day. Versatile, easy and inexpensive — what's not to like?

Vertical Gardening Secrets Revealed

OK, so vertical gardening may be the secret to growing a full year's worth of food in a small space. Don't believe me? No worries...I'm going to teach you how to build a vertical gardening system later in this book.

Vertical gardening isn't suitable for growing all crops, but it works extremely well for some and takes up such a small amount of space that anyone can find space for the design described in Chapter Seven.

Hydroponics Made Easy

Another technique that lends itself well to indoor gardening is known as hydroponics. Hydroponics replaces the conventional soil medium plants are usually grown in with a nutrient-rich water solution which covers the root system of plants. In ideal conditions, hydroponics provides the exact amount of nutrition to a plant and often results in a larger and higher-quality yield.

The problem with many hydroponics systems is cost. Purchasing all the equipment to set up a hydroponic garden in your home could easily cost thousands of dollars. Well, most of the time. In Chapter 7, you'll learn how to build a simple hydroponic system using materials found at the local hardware store.

These are the most common methods used for indoor gardens and I have found that a combination of all these techniques is the best way to consistently grow high-quality food in any space.

Chapter Two: Choosing the Right Soil

Let me start with a question: Do you know the difference between dirt and soil? No worries — let's clear this up quick.

Dirt is simply small pieces of sediment. It could be composed of sand, crushed rock or other inorganic matter. Plants do not grow in dirt (at least not without a lot of help)!

Soil, on the other hand, is full of organic nutrients including naturally decomposed plant matter, essential vitamins and minerals and a host of other things your plants absolutely need to survive.

Creating good soil is like cultivating a garden. It's a constant process that builds upon itself with every passing season. Speaking of which, let's have a conversation about making compost — often called black gold because it's such an effective fertilizer — at home. Specifically, I want to teach you how to make compost inside (without making the house smell nasty).

What is Compost Anyway?

In order to make compost, let's take a moment to understand exactly what compost is and how it benefits the soil.

First… a little history. Composting goes back to the early Roman Empire where organic materials were piled until the next planting season. By then, the material would have decayed enough to be used as a soil amendment.

This method was very successful and required very little input from farmers. The disadvantage of composting this way is that the space is taken up for an entire year, some nutrients might be lost due to rainfall, and unwanted organisms and insects are not properly controlled.

Composting finally became "modernized" in the early 20th century when European farmers began using urban organic materials as fertilizer.

It almost seems like magic, doesn't it? We put a bunch of trash into a pile and suddenly we have chemical free fertilizer that our plants love. Our early ancestors had no idea how the process worked.

All they knew is that it did.

We don't really need to know the science behind composting either. A basic understanding of the process, however, will help us to diagnose future problems accurately.

Modern science has afforded us a look into the composting process. Although we won't spend a lot of time getting into the specifics of how compost is created, this brief overview should help us when we begin making our own compost.

Microorganisms such as bacteria and fungi account for most of the decomposition in a compost pile. These organisms are considered chemical decomposers because they change the actual chemistry of organic wastes.

Conversely, larger organisms such as worms, flies, and a host of other insects are considered physical decomposers because they grind, bite, and chew materials into smaller pieces.

The most important decomposers are known as aerobic bacteria. Although very small, they are extremely important to the composting process. They rely on carbon as a source of energy and nitrogen to build protein in their bodies.

They obtain energy by oxidizing organic material. This oxidation process produces heat. If you have ever seen a compost pile before, you may notice that it is usually warm to the touch. This warmth is created by aerobic bacteria metabolizing carbon in organic matter.

Fungi also play an important part in the decomposition process. Fungi are primitive plants that do not rely on photosynthesis.

Usually, fungi thrive in cooler temperatures with readily available, easily digestible food sources.

As a result, fungi are usually one of the last microorganisms to join the "composting party."

Just as important as the organisms we cannot see are the organisms we can see. Insects and worms breakdown chunks of material into smaller pieces that are more easily digested microorganisms.

There are quite a few macro organisms that are important to the decomposition process for various reasons. For instance, spiders help to control garden pests. Ants help the composting process by bringing fungi and other organisms into their nests. They also help to move minerals around as they work.

By far, the most important macroorganism is the red worm. These worms ingest organic matter and digest it with the help of intestinal juices that are rich in enzymes and other fermenting substances that breakdown the organic material.

They leave behind castings which are rich in plant nutrients such as nitrogen, calcium, and phosphorus. Worms are great for compost piles and for your garden after you have planted.

All of these organisms work together, creating nutrient-rich fertilizer for our plants. Variables such as temperature, moisture, and proper aeration all affect the rate at which these processes occur.

There are many benefits to adding compost to our gardens including:

- Improved Soil Structure – Soil structure refers to the way inorganic particles such as sand and clay combine with decomposed organic particles such as compost. A healthy soil structure is loose and allows for free movement of air, water and nutrients. Compost also helps neutralize the pH of your soil, a very important benefit for some of our more finicky plants.

- Increased Nutrient Content – The aerobic bacteria that are responsible for much of the decomposition process produce nitrites and nitrates (a process call nitrification) that are essential for plant development. Even after compost has been added to the garden, these bacteria will continue to produce these nitrogen-based nutrients for your plants.

- Improved Water Retention – Fertile, healthy soil can retain more water. Adding compost also helps to reduce erosion and runoff. An EPA study shows that soil can retain 16,000 gallons of water more per acre for every 1% of organic material. Obviously, we shoot for much higher than 1% organic material in our soil content so the water retentive abilities of our compost-amended garden are much higher than they would be otherwise.

- Increased Disease Resistance – Studies have shown that compost-amended soil produces plants with fewer pest problems. Studies of tomato plants have proven that compost helps to ward off certain diseases in these and other plant species.

Obviously, there are quite a few benefits to using compost, but if you're overwhelmed at this point, you can use chemical fertilizer or even ready-made compost. If you're still on the proverbial compost train with me, let's breakdown the process of creating compost at home.

You can purchase countertop composting bins from a variety of stores or create your own DIY. Either way, lack of space should not be a concern if you want to create your own nutrient rich soil amendments.

In fact, an excellent indoor composting set up can be constructed using a couple of plastic storage totes.

In the first tote, place a couple of bricks or wooden boards that will act as a spacer. Now take the second tote and drill a few small holes in the bottom.

Place this tote (the one with the holes in the bottom) inside the other tote so it rests on the bricks. You can now add organic material to begin the composting process.

If you compost inside, make sure you turn the compost often. Failure to properly aerate the mixture will result in anaerobic decomposition. It can get extremely smelly; a much more serious concern when you are composting indoors.

On a slightly smaller scale, people have successfully composted inside using plastic peanut jars or coffee cans. The size of your composting bin is dictated by your fertilizer needs and the amount of space you have available.

Mixing it Up

No discussion about compost would be complete without actually discussing what ingredients make up good compost, right?

First, realize that making good compost is all about maintaining the proper ratio of 'green' and 'brown' materials. For best results, strive to maintain a 25:1 ratio of brown to green material.

Brown materials are rich in carbon and include:

- Cardboard (cereal boxes, egg cartons, and paper towel tubes all work well)
- Wastepaper and junk mail (just make sure to remove the plastic window)
- Magazines
- Bedding from some pets (hay, straw, shredded paper, and wood shavings)
- Sawdust
- Wood shavings
- Fruit waste
- Leaves
- Pine needles

Green materials are rich in nitrogen and include:

- Grass cuttings
- Raw vegetable peelings
- Tea bags
- Coffee grounds
- Manure
- Food waste

- Garden waste

You should avoid adding:

- Colored paper (dyes can be toxic)
- Inorganic materials
- Pet droppings (contain several diseases)
- Meat, bones, fish, dairy (they make your compost smell and attract pests)

There are four things that can help speed up the composting process:

- Chop or shred larger items because it makes it easier for bacteria to breakdown. You can use your lawnmower to chop up garden waste and leaves. Use scissors or a paper shredder for cardboard or newspaper.
- Turn and aerate your compost often (at least every couple of days)
- Instead of throwing in small amounts of material constantly, collect waste and add it in one big bunch. This will keep the compost warm and speed the process along.
- Give your compost access to sunlight during the day. This helps to heat up the compost as well. Just be careful because direct sunlight can actually dry out your compost

pile if it becomes too hot. For an indoor compost bin, this is as simple as moving it near a window during the day. When compost is finished, it smells like rich soil. During the process, however, it can smell a little strong at times so you may want to keep your compost sealed.

Please note that if your compost smells really strong, you probably have anaerobic decomposition occurring.

Although this will usually correct itself over time, anaerobic decomposition occurs when helpful aerobic bacteria (which require oxygen) are overrun by their anaerobic counterparts.

Typically, turning over the compost a few times will help to aerate the organic material and allow aerobic bacteria to take over again.

The microorganisms that do most of the work require water. If you add too much water, your organic waste won't decompose properly. Not adding enough water will kill the bacteria and you will never get compost.

Keep in mind that the more green material (such as grass cuttings, weeds, and leaves) you put into the pile, the less water you'll need to add.

The goal is to maintain a moist, but not wet, moisture level in your compost. If you accidentally add too much water, you can add some dry materials such as straw or hay to help absorb the excess water.

Microorganisms also require oxygen. Remember that a lack of oxygen in your compost will result in anaerobic decomposition. We are aiming for aerobic decomposition which means allowing for adequate ventilation in your composting bin.

Seem Like Too Much Work?

Creating your own organic compost is a great way to reuse leftover food items and other waste that typically finds it way into the dumpster. More importantly, however, it gives you complete control over exactly the type of food fed to your plants.

But, I realize that taking on an indoor garden seems like a chore by itself for the uninitiated. That's why we have artificial fertilizer. Sold under a variety of brands (such as Miracle-Gro), these chemical solutions are added to soil at set intervals to give plants required nutrients in less-than-ideal soil.

I'm personally not a proponent of using chemical fertilizer if I can help it, but there's no questioning how much easier it is — especially when just starting out. Eventually, I'm confident that you'll realize the benefits of compost and start your own, but until that day, don't feel bad about taking this shortcut.

And if you're on the fence about using artificial fertilizer but don't have the time to start a compost bin right now, most garden supply stores sell bags of pre-made compost which you can add to your garden; sounds like a win-win situation to me...

Chapter Three: Not All Light is the Same

Ensuring our indoor plants receive enough light is the perpetual challenge for any indoor gardening enthusiast. As I mentioned before, it is possible to give your plants enough natural sunlight that artificial lights aren't required, but this is the exceptional rather than the rule.

Most of us are going to need to at least supplement plants' natural exposure to sunlight and in some cases, such as setting up a garden in a closet, all of the light is artificial.

Knowing how much and what type of light(s) you need is a matter of understanding how much (if any) natural sunlight the plants will receive on a daily basis and the lighting requirements of a particular plant species. While some species of shade leaf lettuce need only 4 -5 hours of sunlight each day, a tomato plant needs at least twice that to produce quality fruit. In fact, that holds true for most fruit-bearing crops you might grow.

We also need to consider the type of light we use. Different types and spectrums of light affect plants differently. For instance, blue light (sometimes referred to as cool light) promotes compact, bushy growth. Red light, on the other hand, induces a hormonal reaction which creates blooms.

Lights that produce an orange or reddish light typically produce a lot of heat — this could be problematic if the lights are too powerful or large for the room or if placed too close to the plants.

I'm not going to lie to you — shopping for grow lights seems like a daunting process. Once you understand the basics, however, it's not really that bad.

For instance, a simple rule to remember is that the less expensive a light is at the time of the purchase, the less efficient (in other words more costly) that light will be when used for your garden.

Now let's take a look at some of the most common lighting options.

Incandescent Bulbs

The least expensive lighting option is the incandescent bulb. These lights work well when placed at least 24" from the plants as they get very hot and can easily burn leaves. Best used with a specific plant or a small grouping of plants, expect the typical incandescent bulb to last around 1,000 hours.

Fluorescent Bulbs

Fluorescent grow lights are probably one of the best choices for a small indoor garden. These bulbs are relatively inexpensive, energy efficient and easy to install. You can expect a fluorescent bulb to provide approximately 20,000 hours of service before requiring replacement.

Most fluorescent light is in the blue spectrum. This encourages bushy plant growth which is perfect for seedlings. Fluorescent light is also cool to the touch meaning it is nearly impossible to damage plants with excessive heat.

Full-Spectrum Fluorescent Bulbs

In addition to providing the blue light of regular fluorescent lights, full-spectrum lights also provide red light to promote more even plant growth.

Modern full-spectrum fluorescent bulbs, such as the T5, are designed to provide triple the output of regular fluorescent lights while remaining energy efficient and long-lasting.

LED Lights

The newest type of grow light on the market is the LED bulb. These bulbs are extremely small and lightweight making them an excellent solution in situations where traditional grow lights and associated fixtures may be too heavy.

LED lights are extremely energy efficient and will last through years of regular use.

High Intensity Discharge (HID) Bulbs

Finally, let's talk about HID bulbs. While certainly one of the most expensive lighting options, HID bulbs are even more powerful than full-spectrum fluorescent bulbs while being even more energy-efficient.

There are two types of HID grow light: metal halide (MH) and high pressure sodium (HPS). MH bulbs tend to emit mostly blue light while HPS lights promote flowering by emitting more red light.

How Much Light Do You Need?

In addition to selecting the type of bulb(s) you want to use for your indoor garden, you also need to know how much light is necessary to support plant growth. Although some plants require more light than others, as a general rule you should plan for 20 - 40 watts per square foot. This has proven to be a sufficient amount of light for most plant species.

Chapter Four: To Water or Not to Water?

Proper watering is one of those mysteries that often seems to elude novice gardeners. It can seem like a constant battle figuring out whether the plants are under- or over-watered.

While each plant has slightly different watering requirements, remember that as a general rule, plants grown in containers dry out faster than plants in a traditional outdoor garden.

You should always use room temperature water and be sure to add enough that water seeps out of the drain holes in the bottom of the container. You can use your finger or a moisture meter to check the moisture level of the soil.

You can also look at the plants to determine whether they are under- or over-watered.

Signs of over-watering include:

- wilting from stems toward leaves
- lower leaves falling off
- stunted growth
- discoloration
- wilting foliage

Signs of under-watering include:

- wilting along the outer edges of leaves
- soil is dry to the touch
- wilting foliage
- leaves and/or flowers dropping prematurely

Also keep in mind that some plants require lots of water, especially when:

- When they are actively growing, i.e. it has young leaves or flower buds.
- If its leaves are thin and delicate and tend to brown at the tips if dry.
- When they are located in warm rooms with direct sunlight.
- If it has many large leaves which transpire heavily.
- If its root mass has filled its pot.
- If it is growing in a relatively small pot.
- If it has been newly propagated.
- If it is growing in dry air (i.e. forced air furnace heating, dry climate).
- If it is native to a bog or marshy area.
- If it is growing in a clay pot.

Just be careful not to over-water as this can also lead to other problems such as root rot and the growth of bacteria and/or fungi which could kill your garden plants.

Hydroponic systems eliminate the need for manual watering by design, which is one of the reasons why it has become such a popular indoor gardening technique. You'll see how easy the system is to operate after we discuss it in Chapter 7.

Chapter Five: The DIY Herb Garden

As I mentioned before, starting an indoor herb garden is one of the easiest ways to learn many of the skills necessary for any indoor gardening project. Herbs tend to be very forgiving compared to other types of plants and with just a few hours of sunlight each day and some water, you should have healthy herbs growing in your home in no time.

While herb gardens can be made from everything from an old shoebox lined with plastic bags to elaborate custom-built windowsill containers, one of my favorite indoor herb gardens uses glass mason jars. Not only is this method extraordinarily easy, it also keeps various herbs separated from one another.

To make a mason jar herb garden, you'll need:

- mason jars (one for each type of herb you want to grow)
- indoor potting soil or a mixture of soil from the yard and compost
- herb seeds
- marker to write the type of herb on the mason jar

That's it! Pretty simple, right?

Start by adding soil to each jar, leaving about two inches of headspace. Add water to the soil until it is moist, but not wet.

Next, add seeds to each container following directions on the package for planting depth.

Add water as needed to keep soil moist but be careful not to over-water as this setup does not allow excess water to drain through the bottom of the container.

These mason jars should be placed on a windowsill where they receive at least five hours of sunlight each day. Again, the directions on the seed packet are an excellent reference for sunlight requirements of a specific herb species.

It won't be long before you have fresh, homegrown herbs ready for harvest. You can use them directly while cooking or dry them out for long-term storage. Either way, it really is that easy to start gardening indoors.

Chapter Six: The Versatility of Vertical Gardening

Earlier we mentioned vertical gardening as a way to grow large amounts of food in a small space. Where a traditional garden is spread out horizontally and takes up a fair amount of space indoors or out, a vertical garden takes advantage of the typically unused space between the ground and the ceiling.

You'll be surprised by how easy vertical gardening can be and how much food you can produce in a space no bigger than a closet.

But Wait...There's More

Space-saving designs are not the only benefit to adopting a vertical gardening strategy. You can also expect to produce much healthier produce in a much faster period of time.

The controlled environment of a vertical gardening setup does not rely on ground soil which can often become depleted of nutrients quickly without an enrichment plan in place.

This controlled environment results in much faster production.

Typically, plants grow to maturity in ½ to 2/3 the time required in conventional gardening techniques.

With complete control of your growing medium and anything that you add to the soil you can rest assured knowing that you are producing 100% organic produce every time. Not only is organic produce healthier but it also commands a much higher price if you ever decided to sell your excess crops.

There are a couple of drawbacks to vertical gardening which we would be wise to discuss before moving on.

In a traditional garden, the ground acts as an insulator against temperature extremes. Although most plants will suffer adversely from prolonged exposure to intense heat or cold, it often takes longer to affect the plants because of the insulating properties of the ground.

In a vertical gardening system, this barrier is not present and subjects your crops to rapid fluctuations in temperature. Obviously this is an issue that affects outdoor vertical gardens more so than indoor setups but can be serious concern if you live in a climate where temperature changes can occur rapidly.

Outdoor gardens offer a degree of autonomy (for short periods of time) that is also not inherent to vertical systems.

Every garden should be watered daily but the ground is very good at holding moisture and providing it to the plants as needed.

This means that your traditional garden will probably be fine if you go on a weekend trip. A vertical garden, on the other hand, needs daily attention and even just a couple of days away from home can severely shock your plants and affect their output.

I'm not saying you will come home to blackened leaves and wilted plants but should be considered before taking a trip. This effect can be mitigated to an extent depending on the vertical gardening design you choose to employ.

The DIY Vertical Garden

Creating a vertical garden at home as a weekend project is extremely simple and very inexpensive.

Many of these can be created with some time and just a few dollars in materials. We will focus on using PVC piping as the basis for our tower.

Once you understand the concepts, the design can easily be adapted for other containers such as plastic garbage cans and buckets.

Materials and tools required for this project include:

- 4 to 6 foot section of 4 inch PVC pipe

- 4 to 6 foot section of ¾ inch PVC pipe

- Potting soil (preferably soil crystals or moisture control soil that will make watering easier)

- Plants – Seedlings will save time over planting seeds in your garden and remove the frustration of planting bad seeds

- Hole saw

- Drill bits of appropriate size

- Electric drill

- A way to stand the tower up securely (there are a few choices here that will be discussed during the construction process)

With materials in hand it is time to begin building your vertical garden. Each garden should only take approximately one hour to assemble from start to finish so you can easily build multiple towers in a single day.

The first step is deciding how tall you want your tower to be. You don't want to be so tall that you have to get on a ladder to harvest crops from the top but you don't want it to be so short that you are missing out on additional vertical space.

Aim for something between 4 and 6 feet tall as this will provide maximum growing room without making care and harvesting extraordinarily difficult.

Take the PVC pipe that you have cut to the desired length based on the mounting method you have chosen and your ideal height for watering (which is done from the top) and harvesting.

Now it's time to cut holes in the pipe where your plants will ultimately grow. To ensure that each plant has enough room to grow, consider staggering the holes in a spiral fashion working from the bottom to the top.

Also take into consideration where you will be growing and the amount of light available to the plants. For instance, if you're putting the garden in a window try to keep all of the plants on the side that will be facing the window. Outdoor installations can typically have plants on all sides of the pipe assuming there is sufficient sunlight.

Each hole should be approximately 2" in diameter and these can be easily cut using a hole saw. These holes can be made larger if the plants you are growing require it but typically 2 inches is enough for most plants to thrive.

When placing your holes also take into account the types of plants you are growing. As already mentioned, plants like strawberries tend to grow down and the spaces between holes should account for this downward growth so as not to thwart the growth of plants on the lower levels of the tower.

If you will be hanging your vertical garden you should also drill a small hole at the bottom of the pipe to allow for drainage. Don't forget to place a catch pan under the hole to collect the drainage.

Once you have cut out all the holes you should use a fine grit sandpaper to smooth the opening of each hole. Not only could sharp edges injure you while you're working with your plants but the edges could also damage root systems and the plants themselves as they begin to grow larger.

Once you're satisfied with the location of all your holes, take the smaller piece of PVC pipe and construct your nutrient distribution "pipeline." Technically, this extra pipe is not needed but once the pipe is filled with soil it will be very hard for the plants at the bottom to receive water and nutrients.

Installing the smaller pipe in the middle ensures that each plant receives nutrients and moisture regardless of where it is positioned in the tower.

Use a small drill bit to drill holes in the small PVC pipe. Spiral designs works best but just make sure that there are enough holes to distribute water evenly throughout the system.

This small pipe can be filled with compost or you can even just use sand to distribute water evenly throughout the system and fertilize in a more conventional way.

Now you are ready to fill your DIY garden tower with soil. Place the smaller pipe into the larger one and use a funnel to fill the larger tube with potting soil. You can wrap the holes in plastic wrap or fabric to prevent spillage of potting soil while you're filling the pipe.

With the tower filled with soil you can now add your seedlings to the system. Use your finger to poke a hole in each of your pre-drilled locations and gently place each seedling into the hole in the potting soil.

Again, if you will be planting strawberries, cucumbers, or any other plant that tends to grow downward try to position these at the bottom with smaller plants or ones that tend to grow upward at the top. This ensures that one species of plant does not inhibit the growth of another.

As you place each seedling into your new garden add a little bit of compost to the hole as well. This will help the little plant get some immediate nutrients until compost nutrients begin to trickle their way down the pipe.

Your new vertical garden is now ready to go and you can begin enjoying the fruits of your labor. The even water distribution of this system allows plants to grow faster and more heartily than they might in a traditional horizontal garden.

Make sure that you water from the top on a regular basis. Water needs to be poured into the smaller tube which will trickle its way down throughout the system allowing plants to wick off moisture as needed.

Additional Tips

Once you have your garden set up, maintaining it is very much the same as traditional gardening methods.

Most plants require at least six hours of sunlight per day and need daily watering. If this is your first attempt at vertical gardening you should probably keep it to one or two setups which can easily be increased with your skill level.

If sunlight is not abundant in your location try to use plants that do well in shade such as lettuce and spinach; both of which can thrive in shady or partial shade conditions.

If you are more interested in growing fruits and sun-loving vegetables but you lack a good location with ample sunlight, you can use artificial lighting.

Try to keep your vertical garden 100% organic. Although it may be tempting to use artificial fertilizers these chemicals are akin to buying produce at the store and spraying it with chemicals at home before consuming it.

Your vertical garden is a closed loop system – meaning that everything you put into the soil ultimately goes into your food and your body.

Chapter Seven: Hydroponics Made Easy

Hydroponics is a gardening technique that uses water instead of dirt to grow plants. The advantage to this system should be immediately obvious. Hydroponic systems do not use dirt; therefore, it can be set up anywhere.

This versatility has many advantages. For those living in apartments or areas where space is limited, a hydroponic setup will allow a small crop to be grown and harvested just about anywhere. In a spare bedroom, on the balcony, or even on the roof of the building are all acceptable places to set up a hydroponic system.

Hydroponic systems take up much less space allowing you to plant more in the same space than you would with a conventional dirt medium. This is because the nutrient rich water is brought directly to the root systems of the plants. The roots will not have to continue growing in search of nutrients so they remain small. Plants will not be fighting for nutrient rich soil and overall the crops tend to be much healthier.

Four Hydroponic Methods to Consider

- Ebb and Flow – An ebb and flow system works by temporarily flooding the root system of your plants and then allowing it to drain. Often, this is one of the least expensive hydroponic setups to get started with and requires a medium amount of care to maintain.

- Nutrient Film Technique (NFT) – NFT is a method of passing a thin stream of nutrient rich water over the root system. Although more expensive to set up initially, it requires less maintenance on a daily basis than the ebb and flow method described above.

- Aeroponics – An off shoot of hydroponics, aeroponics involves suspending your plants in mid-air and spraying a mist of nutrients directly onto the root system. These systems can be made very inexpensively but require the roots to be sprayed very often (if doing so manually) and can be difficult to maintain for this reason.

- Bubbler systems – A bubbler system relies on air bubbles aerating the nutrient solution to keep the root systems moist. It is an effective method that is inexpensive and simple to set up.

Any of these methods will work to get started with hydroponics. It is important to determine exactly where you will be gardening before deciding what method will work best in your situation. If you are devoting the entire basement of your home to your garden, for example, you would be best suited by installing a NFT system. Although the plumbing will be extensive, the time saved in daily maintenance of your garden will pay for itself very quickly.

In a small apartment, ebb and flow systems or even an aeroponics setup will probably be better. It is even possible to create a hanging aeroponics garden in a window that can produce a decent amount of food.

Commercial vs. Homemade Systems

Hundreds of companies offer commercially made hydroponic systems that can have you growing successfully in no time at all. These systems are easy to setup and easy to use. The drawback to using these systems is that they can be very expensive. A small setup for 6-8 plants will cost you over $200 and that does not include the lighting which will be required when growing indoors.

An alternative is to make your own hydroponic system. There are thousands of free plans available on the Internet to construct just about any hydroponic setup you can imagine from large outdoor systems to compact indoor systems designed to fit on a window sill.

If money is not an object in your preparing plans, consider purchasing the necessary equipment from your local hydroponics store. Although expensive, you will save loads of time and be gardening more quickly than you can imagine.

Explain to the employees at the hydroponics store what your goals are and they will be able to direct you to the best equipment for the job. Make sure you know what kind of produce you will be growing and approximately how many plants you will be starting before going to the store. This information is integral to making an informed decision about hydroponic equipment.

The more affordable route is to build your own system especially when you are just starting out. There are many ways to build hydroponic systems at home for pennies compared to the cost of purchasing the same equipment. Below is an example of how to build a simple bubbler system. Although these instructions are for a six plant set up, the materials can easily be adjusted for larger or smaller setups.

Nine Steps to Building and Maintaining a Bubbling Hydroponic Setup

1. Assemble the materials – You will need the following items:
    a. 18 gallon plastic storage bin (with lid)

b. 6 mesh pots (approximately 5" pots will work for most indoor growing)

c. Aquarium air pump – Can be purchased anywhere from Wal-Mart to aquarium supply stores

d. Air stone – For creating bubbles (if you make a bigger setup you will most likely need more than one stone)

e. Air hose – Connects the pump to the air stone

f. 3 gallons of Rockwool Grow Cubes

g. Dyna-Gro or other growing solution

h. Syringe – Makes measuring the growing solution much easier

i. Sharp knife

j. Pencil

2. Place the mesh pots upside down on the lid of the container. Use your pencil to trace around each pot. Make sure to leave an equal amount of space between each of the six circles you have drawn.

Next, trace the bottom of each pot in the center of the circles you just made. Do this carefully so the smaller circle is directly in the center of the larger one.

Now use the knife to cut the smaller circle out of the lid completely. DO NOT cut out the bigger circle. Instead, cut slits from the center (now a hole) to the outer line you made. Doing this will allow the pots to sit snugly into the lid and a better seal will be created.

3. Some storage bins will have breather holes near the top. If not, you will have to cut a small hole above where the water line will be to allow the air tube to run through. Try to make the hole just big enough for the hose. This will help to prevent unwanted sunlight and contaminants from the entering the water.
Follow the instructions for the air stone. Typically, they will need to be rinsed and soaked in water prior to first use. Connect the air stone to the air line and connect the other end to the aquarium pump.

4. Sterilization is important to make sure that only the chemicals you intend are ingested by your garden. Fill the bin with water and add a small amount of bleach. Turn on the air pump and let it run for about a half hour. Dump out all the water and let the bin air dry completely to make sure all the bleach has evaporated.

5. The setup is now ready. The next step is to prepare the growing solution. Fill the bin with water again. Turn on

the air pump and add the proper amount of nutrient solution to the water. If using the 18 gallon bin and Dyna-Grow, you will be using approximately 80 ccs of nutrient solution.

6. Open the bag of Grow Cube or other substrate and use one of the pots to scoop out the material into a large bucket or bowl. If using 6 pots, do this six times. Now fill the bucket of material with water paying attention to how much water you add. Following the growing solution directions again, add the proper amount of nutrient solution to this mixture and mix well. Make sure the growing medium is completely saturated.

    If you will be using plants that have already been started, wash all the dirt from the root system being careful not to damage the roots. Place a small amount of the growing substrate in the bottom of each pot, carefully add the plants, and then fill the pots with the remainder of the substrate. Press the pots into the lid of the container.

7. If you are starting from seeds, you will need seed cubes for them to germinate. The process is the same but you will soak the seed cubes in water, place the seed in the moist cube, and then place them in the main pots. Make sure the top of the seed cube is visible from the top of the

pot. The seeds will require frequent watering until the roots grow and begin feeding from the nutrient solution below.

8. Maintenance – At this point, the setup is complete and the plants should be getting nutrition solely from the solution in the bin. Approximately every two weeks the water will need to be changed in the bin. If this step is omitted the plants will run out of nutrients and toxic byproducts from the plants could stunt their growth or kill them entirely.

   If the water level gets too low between water changes, top it off with clean water. The initial water level should be just below the pots. The roots will extend toward the water. Lower the water level a little. You do not want the roots to become too wet as this can lead to rot and ultimately the death of the plant.

9. The last consideration is lighting for your new hydroponic system. If the bin(s) will be placed next to a window with plenty of natural light, you don't have to worry. However, if you are not this fortunate you will need to invest in some lighting made for plants. They can be put on a timer for automatic control. Make sure the lights are not positioned too closely to the plants as

this can damage them. It is best to talk with a professional about lighting options available for your setup.

This simple system is extremely effective for small indoor gardens. Of course, you could make a bunch of these to grow more food depending on the needs of your family.

Chapter Eight: Making a Miniature Ecosystem

One of the new technologies being leveraged by agricultural communities around the world is known as aquaponics. Aquaponics is a unique solution because it is almost fully self-sufficient and can provide large amounts of high quality food.

Traditional gardens need constant attention and the addition of nutrients on a regular basis to grow properly. Aquaponic systems regulate themselves, allowing for nearly autonomous food production year-round.

What Exactly is Aquaponics?

Aquaponics is a technique that combines many of the benefits of hydroponic setups for growing fresh fruits and vegetables by leveraging fish waste as food for your indoor garden. Not only do you end up with organic produce, you also can harvest fresh fish from the comfort of your own home (depending on the type of fish used).

Hydroponic systems rely on providing nutrient rich water directly to the root systems of plants. Not grown in a soil medium, these plants require elaborate plumbing systems to operate but typically produce higher yields in a shorter period of time than traditional soil farming.

The biggest drawback to hydroponics, however, is the need to add artificial nutrient solutions on a regular basis. Because the plants are not able to draw nutrients from the soil, hydroponic farmers and gardeners need to duplicate these conditions using chemicals that allow the plants to grow.

Aquaponics is very similar to hydroponics in the way nutrients are delivered to the plants. What sets aquaponics apart as a unique, futuristic solution for long-term indoor gardening is the source of the nutrients required by the plants.

Instead of adding synthetic chemical solutions to water, aquaponics systems rely on fish waste to produce yields that can be as much as four times larger than traditional growing methods.

Fish excrete solid waste as well as ammonia through their breathing process. In their natural state, these waste products are not beneficial to plant life. However, aquaponics systems rely on helpful bacteria to convert ammonia into nitrates and nitrites that can be used by the plants as food.

An aquaponics system has a variety of components inherent to its design that mimic the natural order of the ecosystem throughout the world.

Fish tanks are used to house fish while they grow to maturity. These fish are fed on a daily basis and produce solid waste and ammonia as byproducts of their metabolic process.

A pump moves this water at a regular interval from the fish tanks into the grow beds of the system. These grow beds are filled with inert medium such as crushed granite, expanded clay, or a variety of synthetic materials.

The ammonia-rich water floods the grow beds. Aerobic bacteria digest ammonia and produce nitrogen-based products as part of the metabolic process; leaving these helpful plant nutrients in the growing medium.

Worms are usually added to the growing medium as well. These animals are able to break down solid fish waste into usable plant food as a result of their metabolic process.

A drainage system allows water to drain back into the fish tank. The digestive processes that occur in the grow bed convert the ammonia enriched water (which is harmful to fish in large concentrations) into nitrates used by the plants. These nitrates are harmless to the fish.

The process that occurs in the grow bed acts like a biofilter making the water suitable for the fish. This constant cycle of filtration and conversion mimics natural processes and represents a truly sustainable option for producing food.

The Benefits of Aquaponics

Aquaponics offers many benefits over other gardening techniques.

Aquaponics allows plants and fish to live harmoniously without producing any unusable waste. That is the true mark of a sustainable solution. You put very little into the system and reap tremendous benefits.

By its very design, aquaponics creates 100% organic produce that is not impregnated with chemical additives or insecticides. In fact, adding these chemicals to an aquaponics system will kill the helpful bacteria that are integral to the conversion process and the system will fail.

These bacteria are what create the self-sufficient ecosystem.

Although they can be introduced synthetically to speed up the creation of the biofilter, this is often unnecessary as high levels of ammonia will allow the bacteria to grow on their own. Once an aquaponics system has a healthy population of bacteria, they will reproduce and maintain their numbers automatically.

As long as the bacteria population is healthy, an aquaponics system only needs new fish as mature ones are harvested and plants to continue absorbing the nitrogen products created by the bacteria.

Aquaponics uses much less water than traditional gardening or hydroponic systems. Because the system is designed as a closed loop, the only water lost is small amounts absorbed by plant material and evaporative processes.

The Specifics of an Aquaponics System

With a general overview of how aquaponics systems work, we can now take a look at the specific components of a functional system.

Fish tanks are where the fish live, eat, and reproduce. Most systems have several fish tanks to accommodate different sized animals. This is especially important for carnivorous species that may eat smaller fish.

Once the fish population has reproduced, the fingerlings should be moved to a separate tank where they can grow without threat from larger fish.

The size of the fish tank is completely dependent on the overall size of the system. The capacity of the fish tank should be a close match to the capacity of the grow beds.

This ensures that the entire water system is properly filtered to remove contaminants from the fish habitat. Tanks from 10 gallons to 1,000 gallons or more have been successfully used in aquaponics systems. Obviously, the costs increase with the size of the tank but the production is also increased.

Fish tanks are generally plastic but can also be made out of glass. Many people have successfully used outdoor swimming pools, large pond liners, and even large plastic containers to house fish.

Grow beds are where your plants will live and should be sized to accommodate the water held in the fish tank.

Typically, grow beds should be large enough to hold approximately 12 inches of growing medium. About 10 inches of this should be flooded with water leaving a dry barrier of approximately 2 inches near the top of the grow bed. This dry layer helps to insulate the bacteria population below from the atmosphere and reduces the likelihood that plants will become damaged from excess water during a period of flooding.

Grow beds can be made from a variety of materials but the most common is plastic. High-grade plastic is durable, lightweight, and reduces the likelihood of introducing foreign contaminants into the system that could have an adverse effect on pH levels.

This strategy should also be followed when selecting fish tanks. Metal enclosures as well as some types of plastic can produce wild fluctuations in the water composition. This can result in poor production or even no production at all if left unchecked.

The growing medium is where your plants will establish root systems and where your bacteria population will call home.

Growing medium needs to be completely inert to be effective. Just as cheap materials used for grow beds or fish tanks can adversely affect water conditions, so can cheap growing medium. A popular growing medium is crushed granite because it is inert and easy to source.

If you choose to use crushed granite, make sure it does not contain any limestone. Even in small concentrations, limestone will have a perpetual effect on the pH of your system and make the aquaponics system unstable.

Expanded clay is also popular and can be purchased in large quantities for relatively cheap. Once again, the issue becomes the long-term sustainability and availability of these products in the future.

Fortunately, growing medium does not need to be replaced assuming you selected an inert material that does not break down over time. The only time new growing medium may be required is if you choose to expand your aquaponics system in the future.

We know that water must be pumped from the fish tanks to the grow beds on a regular basis for this miniature ecosystem to be successful.

This is done almost exclusively using electric pumps. A sump pump or outdoor pond pump are the two most popular methods of moving water within the aquaponics system. Some may consider this to be a weak point in the sustainability of aquaponics because there is a risk for mechanical failure of these parts.

The fact that they are relatively inexpensive tends to negate this potential drawback simply because stocking a reasonable supply of replacement pumps is not difficult or expensive.

Pumps can be configured in a number of ways depending on the exact system being designed. The most common, and easily implemented system, is known as ebb and flow.

A full flood and drain cycle should be completed approximately every hour. Ideally, this is accomplished by a 15 minute, pump on flood session and 45 minutes of slow draining through the growing medium and back into the fish tanks. There are a couple of common methods to automate this process.

Timers are often used to regulate when the pump is on and the grow bed is being flooded. A timer set to flood the grow beds every 15 minutes can be a simple mechanical timer or a more advanced electronic one.

When the timer is on, the pump operates and moves water between the fish tank and the grow bed. When the pump is off, the water begins to slowly drain back into the tank.

Another common method is known as a siphon tube. A siphon tube is a simple device that automatically siphons water back to the fish tank once a certain water level has been reached in the grow bed.

These can be constructed very easily at home or purchased relatively inexpensively through aquaponics supply stores. A siphon tube make sure that the water level in the grow bed gets high enough without overflowing and does not stop siphoning water until the grow bed is empty. When the grow bed is empty, air enters the siphon tube and stops the siphoning action.

In this design, the pump always runs which is usually better for the internal components than abrupt starting and stopping associated with using a mechanical or electrical timer.

The plumbing components of an aquaponics system vary greatly but should follow the same rules about using inert materials as the rest of the system.

PVC piping is by far the most popular solution because it is easy to source, easy to manipulate, and lasts for a long time without introducing harmful contaminants into the aquaponics system.

In addition to the PVC piping, which will vary in size and length depending on the specific application, a variety of connectors will also be required.

Probably the best connector for PVC piping entering and exiting grow beds and fish tanks is the bulkhead connector.

By using a silicone seal and a threaded end, bulkhead connectors offer watertight seals that are much more reliable than slip-on connectors.

Another major component of a successful aquaponics system is the organisms that make biofiltration possible.

Helpful bacteria that convert ammonia into nitrogen-based nutrients that plants can use are a necessary part of the filtration process.

These bacteria will grow and reproduce autonomously provided there is an ammonia-enriched environment. Once the bacteria population has established itself, it is self-regulating. The bacteria stop producing once they have reached their maximum population given the amount of available nutrients.

The bacteria that make up the biofilter in an aquaponics system take time to establish when a new system is created.

This is known as cycling in the aquaponics world. Establishing a healthy biofilter is important for both the fish and the plants. *Cycling can be done in two ways:*

- With Fish
- Without Fish

Each cycling method presents a unique set of advantages and disadvantages that should be considered when creating your biofilter.

First, let's look at cycling with fish.

This is probably the easier of the two methods because once the aquaponics system has been set up you simply add fish and allow their natural ammonia production to bring bacteria into the system.

The downside to cycling with fish is that the ammonia levels will often get too high for many of the fish to survive before the bacteria population is strong enough to counteract ammonia production.

If you choose to cycle with fish you should consider using an inexpensive species such as goldfish for cycling. This will be much less expensive than stocking your tank with tilapia or other edible species only to have a portion of them die.

Cycling without fish eliminates the risk to the animals but typically takes a little bit longer to generate a healthy bacteria population.

A setup aquaponics system is run continuously while ammonia is added artificially to the system. You can use pure ammonia (make sure it's not the sudsy kind) or you can even urinate in the fish tank as human urine contains a high concentration of ammonia.

Either way, ammonia needs to be added daily until testing confirms that the ammonia level coming back to the tank is significantly less than the ammonia level in the tank.

This is a good indication that a healthy bacteria population has arrived and is successfully processing ammonia into nitrogen-based nutrients. At this time, it is safe to add fish without fear of exposing them to unnecessarily high levels of ammonia.

The other aspect of successful aquaponics is vermiculture. Vermiculture is adding worms to your system for natural composting of organic waste.

While the bacteria work to break down the ammonia-enriched water of the system, the worms will digest the solid waste introduced to the grow beds and create compost tea.

The worms will thrive in the growing media even with the high moisture content. Worms and bacteria combine to make up a perfect biofiltration system that never needs to be changed and ensures your plants are receiving maximum nutrition all the time.

Plants to Grow

Aquaponics systems are very versatile in that just about any type of produce imaginable can be grown successfully.

People have actually grown banana trees exclusively in an aquaponics environment. Even carrots and other subterranean produce can be grown successfully.

Keep in mind that you may have some interesting looking carrots as the aquaponic growing medium is usually less forgiving than soil; forcing the plants to take unusual shapes. Rest assured, however, that these vegetables will taste just as good as their traditionally grown (and shaped) counterparts.

Due to the nature of aquaponics system, plants can be much closer together than typically experienced in traditional growing environments. Coupled with the much higher yields (as much as four times more per plant), it is easy to see why aquaponics is a sustainable and powerful solution for long-term food production.

DIY Aquaponics System

In the beginning, especially during cycling, it can be tricky to learn the ropes of an aquaponics system so it is best to start with a small system that can be grown as your skill levels improve.

Once the system has been established, however, there is very little daily maintenance required to grow produce successfully.

The cost of an aquaponics system is completely dependent on the size. The larger the system, the more expensive the grow beds, fish tanks, pumps, and plumbing apparatus will become.

A smaller system can easily be scaled in the future by adding additional grow beds and fish tanks (which should be kept at a 1:1 ratio in most circumstances).

Let's take a look at what would be required to set up a small system that could be successfully operated within your home. A common list of materials might include:

- 50 gallon stock tank – These can be purchased from a farm supply store and are used to water livestock. They are made of durable plastic and can house a good number of fish.

- 30 gallon capacity grow bed – The grow bed needs to be deep enough to accommodate approximately 12 inches of growing medium and have a capacity that can hold most of the fish tank capacity. In this case, about ½ the fish tank capacity can be held in the grow bed after growing medium.

  The grow bed should be made out of inert plastic and be sturdy enough to support the weight of water and growing medium. You can look around at hardware stores for plastic totes or small kiddie pools that may work well for this purpose. Garden stores sell purpose-built grow beds, although these typically are more expensive.

- PVC piping – This is the circulatory system of your aquaponics set up. All the water in the system will flow through this piping between the fish tanks and the grow beds. The amount of piping you need depends on the exact configuration you choose to employ (grow bed and fish tank next to each other versus on top of each other).

- Outdoor Pond Pump – A pond pump works well to move water from the fish tank to the grow beds. They are designed to last for years with no maintenance and use a very small amount of electricity to operate.

  Make sure that the flow rate of the pump is sufficient for the size of your fish tank. In this example, we would need a pump with a flow rate of approximately 200 gallons per hour. We want most of the water in the fish tank to be pumped into the grow bed within about a 15 minute span while allowing for about 45 minutes of drainage time before the next cycle begins.

- Growing Media – The growing media can be many different materials but for this example, let's use expanded clay which is commonly available from many gardening supply stores.

It is lighter than crushed granite and there is no risk of adding limestone or other potentially harmful elements to the ecosystem.

- Fish – In this closet sized example, we will be using goldfish. They are inexpensive and hearty enough to survive cycling with fish. This species could easily be swapped out for bluegill or another small edible species.
- Plants – Any plant can be grown successfully using this method so it will ultimately be your decision. For the purposes of this example, we will assume that the system is located next to a window that provides at least six hours of natural sunlight per day.
  If your system will actually be in a closet or in a window that does not receive much direct sunlight, you may need to include artificial lighting into your project.

- Mechanical Timer – A cheap mechanical timer from the hardware store will control when the pump turns on and off. It should be set to activate the pump for 15 minutes every hour so the grow beds have ample time to drain before the next flood cycle.

Constructing the System

With all the materials collected, we can begin assembling our small aquaponics system.

To simplify construction of this design, we will be placing the fish tank directly below the grow bed. With a few small holes placed in the bottom of the grow bed, the drainage will automatically fall back into the fish tank.

The holes should not be too big. This ensures that the water is properly filtered before returning to the fish tank.

An overflow tube made of PVC should be installed at the maximum water line in the grow bed. This prevents the grow bed from overflowing and from too much water leaving the fish tank and suffocating the fish during the flood cycle.

Fill the grow bed with expanded clay and position it above the fish tank. Since this design is relatively lightweight, the grow bed can sit directly on top of the fish tank without any concern for collapse.

Connect the flexible tubing that comes with the pond pump to a small straight section of PVC pipe approximately 3/4" thick that goes into a hole drilled in the grow bed. This connection should be secured with a bulkhead style connector. When assembling the connector, make sure the silicone seal is flat to avoid leaks.

Connect the timer to the electrical connection of the pump and set the timer to operate 15 minutes out of every hour.

Fill the fish tank with water and test the operation of the pump. Most pond pumps have an adjustable flow rate and you may need to adjust the flow to balance out the flooding and draining. There is no real formula for this. Trial and error works best.

The grow bed should flood fully without overflowing during the 15 minute interval that the pump is running and it should not drain too quickly because this doesn't allow the water enough time to be properly filtered.

Once you have adjusted the flow rate appropriately, you can add your goldfish safely.

In a 50 gallon tank, 50 to 60 small goldfish will produce plenty of ammonia without being overcrowded in the tank.

At this time, you can also add seedlings to the grow bed so that as the bacteria begin to convert ammonia into nitrogen-based nutrients, they can begin to grow.

Keep in mind that this is a simplified design that, although effective, leaves much to be desired as far as reliability and autonomy.

This very basic system demonstrates the effectiveness of aquaponics on a small scale. It works perfectly for a small indoor garden and provides all the benefits of a hydroponic system without using chemical fertilizers.

Chapter Nine: Top 10 Indoor Gardening Tips & Tricks

Now that you understand some of the ways we can successfully grow fruits, vegetables and herbs in the comfort of our own homes, I wanted to share some tips with you that I've picked up over the years that help to summarize some of the things we have already discussed.

1. Indoor plants always tend to grow toward a light source It could be the window near the garden or the artificial grow lights. Either way, keep this in mind when setting up the garden and try to keep all plants equidistant from light sources when possible to promote vertical growth. If you notice your plants started to bend to one side or the other, consider rotating them to compensate.

2. Always make sure indoor plants receive enough light. Whether from a window, an artificial grow light or both, plants need a minimum of five hours of sunlight each day and some varieties require double that to bear fruit.

3. More plants die from improper watering than any other problem. Follow the chapter about watering to make sure your plants are getting exactly the right amount of water. Of course, in hydroponic and aquaponic systems,

watering is automatic but this is not the case in container gardens.

4. Don't be afraid to clean your plants from time to time. Wiping down leaves keeps dust and debris from accumulating and results in healthier, more robust plants.

5. Remember that your plants need adequate airflow to flourish. Stale, stagnant air will adversely affect plant growth. If natural airflow isn't present, use a small fan to move air over and through the garden.

6. Be mindful of temperature. Ideally, the temperature in your home should be around 70°F during the day and approximately 10° colder at night. This mimics the conditions of plants in outdoor gardens.

7. Keep records of what you have planted, when you planted it and what type of fertilizer was used. You can also monitor which plants do best near other plants. As you develop this system, you will notice trends which can be used to maximize production in future years.

8. Make sure your plants are getting enough food. Especially in container gardens, every time you water some nutrients are flushed from the soil. Either add small amounts of liquid fertilizer or add more compost to maintain the nutrient level required for optimum growth.

9. Choose the right soil. Using soil directly from outside usually results in weeds and bacteria being introduced to the indoor growing medium. Use purpose-built potting soil or organic compost for best results.

10. Ensure your containers have proper drainage to avoid root rot and other problems usually associated with poor drainage.

Chapter Ten: Choosing the Right Plants

As I've said before, when done properly, indoor gardening is capable of supporting any type of plant that can be grown outdoors. The trick is to use the right container for the crop. You also need to make sure all plant requirements (such as light and airflow) are met for the particular species.

That said, there are some plants that work especially well in indoor environments.

Vertical Gardening Crops

This list is not meant to be all-inclusive but rather a glimpse into some of the more popular vegetables that are easily grown in a vertical manner.

- Peppers
- Lettuce
- Radishes
- Onions
- Eggplant
- Potato
- Assorted Herbs

A variety of climbing plants can also thrive in a vertical garden including:

- Cucumber
- Squash
- Tomato
- Green beans
- Peas

If you choose to grow any of these varieties, make sure to have a support system already in place before planting seeds or seedlings.

Although it is certainly more labor-intensive to create a support structure for your vertical garden some plants, such as beans, consistently produce as much as 10 times more than a bush bean.

A variety of fruits can also be grown using a vertical garden with strawberries being one of the most popular. If you choose to grow strawberries just make sure that you leave enough space between plants in your tower because strawberries tend to grow down and could interfere with the production of plants below them.

While the crops above work well for vertical gardening, they can also be grown in containers or hydroponic systems quite easily.

Other plants that are easy to cultivate and do well indoors include:

- Tomatoes
- Potatoes
- Onions
- Carrots
- Bell peppers
- Leeks
- Raspberries
- Cabbage
- Cauliflower
- Broccoli
- Asparagus
- Celery
- Sage
- Savory
- Parsnips
- Lettuce
- Strawberries
- Summer squash
- Zucchini
- Basil

One of the most exciting parts of indoor gardening is experimenting with new crops and techniques. Please do not use the list above as your only reference. With a little planning and research, it is possible to grow anything indoors.

Use your imagination. Grow things you actually want to eat and reap the benefits of gardening indoors no matter how much — or how little — space you have available.

Made in the USA
Lexington, KY
05 February 2017